DADDY,
HOW DO PLANES FLY?

by Chris Ryan Miller

Dedication

This book is dedicated to my dad who gave me the spirit of giving. His legacy lives on in the countless family and friends he touched.

Glenn Miller
June 13, 1955 - November 18, 2020

How do planes fly?

Planes are able to fly because of their big wings, powerful engines, horizontal tail, vertical tail, and pilots.

The shape of a plane's wings
generates LIFT.
It's the same as if I were to
LIFT you up into the air.

4

AIR

 LIFT

The direction and speed of the airflow creates **LIFT** on the wings.

6

The engines provide **THRUST**. Thrust pushes the airplane forward through the sky.
The **THRUST** helps to **LIFT** the wings.

7

THRUST

8

This is the **VERTICAL** tail.

The rudder on the **VERTICAL** tail points the nose of the airplane left and right.

The left and right motion is called **YAW**.

12

This is the **HORIZONTAL** tail.

14

The **HORIZONTAL** tail points the nose of the airplane up and down. The up and down motion is called **PITCH**.

16

Together the vertical and horizontal tails make up the EMPENNAGE.

18

The **AILERONS** on the wings rotate the plane over.

19

20

The rotating motion is called ROLL.

22

With instrumentation pilots control the wings and engines as well as the horizontal and vertical tails.

The buttons and switches in front of the PILOTS make up the INSTRUMENTATION.

24

The pilots use the INSTRUMENTATION to guide the plane through the sky. Pilots get us where we need to go!

Who can be pilots?

Both boys and girls can become pilots and fly airplanes. YOU could be a pilot.

Now we know how planes fly!

About the Author

The inspiration for writing children's books came from Chris Ryan Miller's very own passion and enthusiasm for flight. As a child, he was exposed to the aviation industry by his father, who has worked in the field for over 25 years. Growing up, they spent evenings watching airplanes take-off and land from the observation area outside Lambert St. Louis Airport. Chris also spent numerous hours on the computer playing Microsoft Flight Simulator with thoughts of one day piloting his own aircraft.

Chris opting for a career with both feet on the ground entered Tuskegee University eager to pursue a career in Aerospace Engineering. He chose to attend Tuskegee University for its distinction of training the famed Tuskegee Airmen, which were also inspirational in his choice of careers. Since graduating from Tuskegee University Chris Ryan Miller has taken a keen interest to inspire children to follow their dreams through his books and mobile flight simulator.

www.ingramcontent.com/pod-product-compliance
Lightning Source LLC
Chambersburg PA
CBHW040249100426
42811CB00011B/1202